HOW-TO SPORTS

SOCCER

Paul Joseph
ABDO & Daughters

Published by Abdo & Daughters, 4940 Viking Drive, Suite 622, Edina, Minnesota 55435.

Copyright © 1996 by Abdo Consulting Group, Inc., Pentagon Tower, P.O. Box 36036, Minneapolis, Minnesota 55435 USA. International copyrights reserved in all countries. No part of this book may be reproduced in any form without written permission from the publisher.

Printed in the United States.

Cover Photo credits: Archive Photos
Interior Photo credits: Archive Photos, pages 5, 12, 15, 25
Superstock, pages 10, 17, 19, 21, 27

Edited by Bob Italia

Library of Congress Cataloging-in-Publication Data

Joseph, Paul, 1970-
    Soccer / Paul Joseph
      p. cm. -- (How-To Sports)
    Includes index.
    Summary: Explains how to play soccer, with discussion of the basic positions as well as such plays as kicking, passing, dribbling, heading, and trapping.
      ISBN 1-56239-649-8
    1. Soccer--Juvenile literature. [1. Soccer.] I. Title. II. Series:
    GV943.25.J67 1996   96-1633
    796.334--dc20   CIP
                                                                          AC

Contents

The Game of Soccer

The main object of soccer is to **kick** the ball in the other team's **goal** and to stop them from scoring. Each goal is worth one point. At the end of the game, the team with the most points wins the game.

Soccer is the most widely played and most watched team sport in the world. Hundreds of millions of fans follow it.

Soccer is played mainly with the feet. Only the **goalie**, within the goal area, may touch the ball with his or her hands.

The game began in the middle 1800s in England. By 1855, soccer clubs were established and the sport gained popularity all through **Europe**.

Soccer is the most widely played and watched team sport in the world.

In 1869, soccer made it to the United States. Two college teams, Princeton and Rutgers, played what people have said was the first American football game. But the game was really a soccer match!

To play the game of soccer well and to have fun, you should learn all you can about the game. **Kicking**, **passing**, **dribbling**, and other basics are all parts of the game. Once you learn these skills, you will see why soccer is the most popular game in the world.

The Field

The game of soccer is played by teams on a **field**. A soccer field is a little bigger than a football field. Fields range in size from 100 to 130 yards (91 to 120 m) long and 50 to 100 yards (46 to 91 m) wide.

The field is divided into two sections. A **center line** divides the field in half. The **center circle** in the middle of the field is used for **kickoffs** at the beginning of a game and after a **goal** is scored.

At each end there is a goal. Each team tries to get the ball into the other team's goal.

The **sidelines** on each side mark the **boundaries**. If the ball touches or crosses these lines, the ball is "dead" and the other team gets the ball. The same holds true for the lines at each end of the field.

Kicking

The main skill all soccer players need is **kicking**. It is used to move the ball from one player to another or to score a **goal**.

To kick the ball, swing your kicking foot back, then kick the ball very hard with the side of your foot. Swing your leg all the way through. Remember to keep your eye on the ball.

When kicking a ball, you want to have power and hit the target. The best way to control your kicking is to kick the ball with the inside of your foot.

It is important to practice kicking. Practice with other players or by yourself. If you are practicing by yourself, find a wall to kick against. Make a target on the wall and aim for it. Begin by shooting from short distances until you repeatedly hit the target, then move back farther.

You can practice with other people by **kicking** it back and forth to each other. Another good way to practice is to have someone bounce the ball to you and you try to kick it. Because the soccer ball often bounces on the field, a player must be good at kicking a bouncing ball.

Kicking is very important in soccer, but you must also learn other skills to be a good, all-around player.

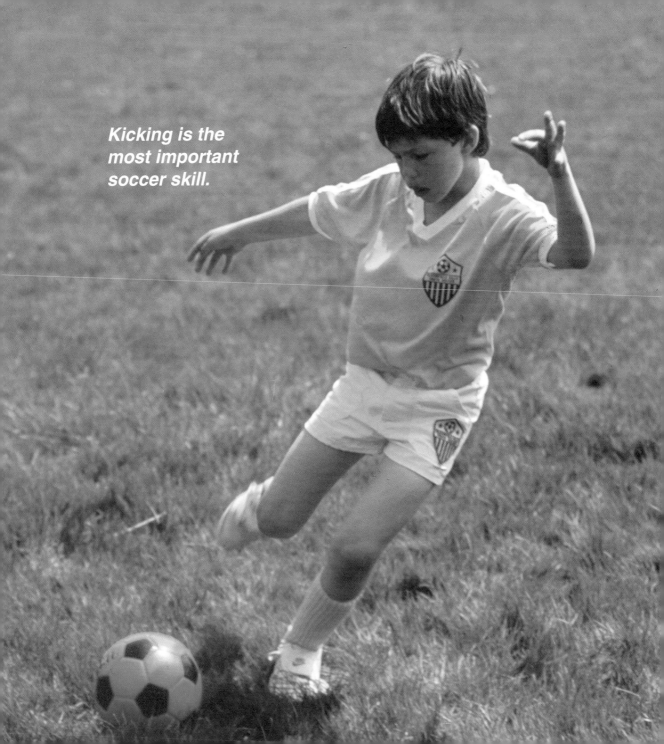

Kicking is the most important soccer skill.

Passing

To get the ball to another player, you must **pass** it. A player can do this by **kicking**, pushing, or **heading** the ball. Before passing, you must decide where you want the ball to go. You may want to pass it down the **field** or only a few feet (meters).

Once you know where you want the pass to go, you must think about the right way to move the ball. The best way to pass is to use the large, flat part of the inside of your foot. This part will give you more control.

Raise your foot off the ground, even with the center of the ball. Swing your foot forward so that it hits the center of the ball. Make sure to follow through in a straight line.

Practice is the key to being a good passer. The best way to practice is to **pass** back and forth to a friend. Every so often, move back so you can practice passing from many distances.

To be a good passer, you must know how to move the ball with both feet. When practicing, always use both feet.

Soccer players use the dribble to move the ball downfield.

Dribbling

In soccer, players **dribble** the ball much like players dribble in basketball. The main difference is that in soccer, players use their feet. In both sports, players dribble so they can eventually **shoot** and score.

Soccer players use the dribble to move the ball downfield. Players can dribble around someone **guarding** them when there is no one to **pass** to.

When dribbling, keep the ball close and use the insides or outsides of your feet. Keep your head up. You must know where your **opponents** are at all times. You also must watch for your own **teammates** so you can pass the ball to them.

It takes practice to become a good dribbler. You must learn how to change direction quickly and start up at different times.

Heading

Heading is another way to move the ball. You do this by hitting the ball with your forehead. If the ball is too high to **kick**, you can either **pass** the ball to a teammate with a "head" pass, or you can try to score by knocking the ball into the **goal** with your head.

When heading, always keep your eye on the ball. As it comes toward you, hit the ball with your forehead. If you hit the ball properly, your forehead will not get hurt.

Opposite page:
This player is using his
head to advance the ball.

Trapping

During a soccer game, sometimes you must stop the ball in the air or on the ground. This is called **trapping**. You "trap" the ball to get control so you can **pass**, **dribble**, or **shoot**.

A player can trap the ball by letting it hit the chest, knee, or thigh so that the ball drops to the ground. Then the ball can be trapped with the foot.

Remember not to use your hands or arms to trap the ball. If you do, you will get a **penalty**.

Opposite page:
A player practicing trapping.

The Throw-In

The **throw-in** is used by players when the ball goes out of bounds. If someone **dribbles**, **passes**, or **kicks** a ball out of bounds by crossing the **sidelines** or **endlines**, the other team gets a "throw-in." This is the only time a player (besides a **goalie**) can use the hands without getting a **penalty**.

To do a throw-in, keep both feet on the ground behind the sideline. Hold the ball behind your head so it touches the back of your neck. Then bring the ball over your head and release it.

The purpose of this move is to throw the ball to someone on your team so they can dribble, pass, or **shoot** for a **goal**. You want to throw away from the other team.

The player who throws the ball in cannot be the first player to touch the ball. It must touch another player first before the throw-in player can touch it.

Preparing for a throw-in, a player looks for a teammate.

Positions

In the game of soccer, there are two teams on the **field**. Each team has 11 players. There is an **offensive team**, which is the team that is trying to score, and a **defensive team**, which is trying to stop the other team from scoring.

A basic set up for each team has four **forwards**, two **midfielders**, four **defenders**, and a **goalie**.

The forwards' main job is to score. They should be good **shooters** and **dribblers**. The midfielders' job is to help score by getting the ball to the forwards. They have to be good **passers**.

The main job of the defenders is to keep the other team from having a good shot at the **goal**. They play in front of the goalie and try to steal the ball from the other team. The defenders must be able to handle and control the ball. Once they get the ball, they often pass to a **midfielder** to start the offensive **attack**.

The **goalie's** job is to keep the ball from going in the **goal**. The goalie is the only player who can use

the hands or arms to catch or block the ball. The goalie also must direct the **defenders**, and be able to **kick** or throw the ball a long way.

A goalie protects the goal.

How-To
Soccer

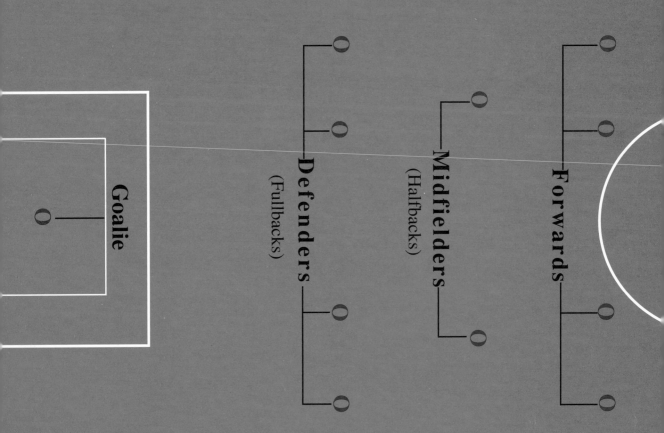

Goalie

Defenders
(Fullbacks)

Midfielders
(Halfbacks)

Forwards

Up to 130 yards (119 m) long

X
X
Forwards
X
X

X
Midfielders
(Halfbacks)
X

X
X
Defenders
(Fullbacks)
X
X

Up to 100 yards (91 m) wide

Goalie
X

Playing the Game

Now that you know the basics of soccer, you can start playing. The best way to play soccer is to keep all players involved in the game. A good team has all 11 players working together.

Everybody on the team can be a part of scoring a **goal**. The play may begin with the **goalie kicking** or throwing to one of the **defenders**. They may **pass** it to one of the **midfielders**. Then the midfielder may try to pass the ball to a **forward** who will **shoot**—and maybe score.

If the other team has control of the ball, you must work hard to get it back. To be a good, all-around soccer player, you must be able to play defense as well as **offense**.

Everybody on the team can be a part of a scoring play.

Fair Play and Team Spirit

Soccer is a total team sport. Every position is important. No one or two players can win a game. It takes everyone playing together—and playing hard.

Support your teammates throughout the game—even when they make bad plays. And if you lose, congratulate your **opponents**. This will make soccer more rewarding—and a lot more fun!

If you practice the basics and work hard at the game, you will see why soccer is the most popular team sport in the world.

Glossary

attack - when the offensive team has the ball and is going downfield to try to score.

boundaries - lines or areas that players or the ball cannot pass.

center circle - a circle in the middle of the field that is used for kickoffs.

center line - a line that divides the field in half.

defender - the player who plays back and helps the goalie by not letting a good shot get off by the other team.

defensive team - the team that does not have control of the ball and is trying to stop the other team from scoring.

dribble - having control of the ball with your foot and continuing to move downfield.

endlines - the lines on both ends of the field that determine the boundaries.

Europe - a continent that has many countries, such as France, Sweden, Great Britain, Italy, etc. It is west of Asia and East of the Atlantic Ocean.

field - the area where the game of soccer is played.

forward - a player who is up front and whose main job is to score.

goal - a point awarded to a team that scores. It is also the netted area where players try to shoot the ball.

goalie - the player whose main job is to stop the ball from going into the goal.

guard - staying close to a player on the other team and trying to get the ball away from them.

heading - hitting the ball with the forehead.

kicking - using the foot to move the ball to another player, downfield, or to shoot.

kickoff - putting the ball in motion at the beginning of the game and after a goal is scored.

midfielder - a player who is stationed in the middle of the field and is a good dribbler and passer.

offensive team - the team that has control of the ball and is trying to score.

opponent - a player on the other side in a game.

pass - to kick, head, or push the ball to a teammate.

penalty - when a player does something against the rules.

shoot - to send the ball toward the goal while scoring or trying to score.

sidelines - the lines on each side of the field that determine the boundaries.

teammates - other players that are on your team.

throw-in - throwing the ball onto the field from the sideline after the ball has gone out of bounds by the other team.

trapping - stopping the ball in the air or on the ground and then controlling it by putting your foot on top of it.

Index